Greater Than a T

Reviews f,

I think the series is wonderful and beneficial for tourists to get information before visiting the city.

-Seckin Zumbul, Izmir Turkey

I am a world traveler who has read many trip guides but this one really made a difference for me. I would call it a heartfelt creation of a local guide expert instead of just a guide.

-Susy, Isla Holbox, Mexico

New to the area like me, this is a must have!

-Joe, Bloomington, USA

This is a good series that gets down to it when looking for things to do at your destination without having to read a novel for just a few ideas.

-Rachel, Monterey, USA

Good information to have to plan my trip to this destination.

-Pennie Farrell, Mexico

Great ideas for a port day.

-Mary Martin USA

Aptly titled, you won't just be a tourist after reading this book. You'll be greater than a tourist!

-Alan Warner, Grand Rapids, USA

Thank you for a fantastic book.

-Don, Philadelphia, USA

Even though I only have three days to spend in San Miguel in an upcoming visit, I will use the author's suggestions to guide some of my time there. An easy read - with chapters named to guide me in directions I want to go.

-Robert Catapano, USA

Great insights from a local perspective! Useful information and a very good value!

-Sarah, USA

This series provides an in-depth experience through the eyes of a local. Reading these series will help you to travel the city in with confidence and it'll make your journey a unique one.

-Andrew Teoh, Ipoh, Malaysia

GREATER THAN A TOURIST – BOSTON MASSACHUSETTS USA

50 Travel Tips from a Local

Alexander J. Dunn

Cover designed by:Lisa Rusczyk Ed. D.
Cover Image: https://pixabay.com/en/boston-massachusetts-skyline-1099418/

Edited by: Linda Fitak

Greater Than a Tourist
Visit our website at www.GreaterThanaTourist.com

Lock Haven, PA
All rights reserved.
ISBN: 9781981098989

>TOURIST

50 TRAVEL TIPS FROM A LOCAL

BOOK DESCRIPTION

Are you excited about planning your next trip?

Do you want to try something new?

Would you like some guidance from a local?

   If you answered yes to any of these questions, then this Greater Than a Tourist book is for you.

   Greater Than a Tourist- Boston Massachusetts USA by Alexander J. Dunn offers the inside scoop on Boston. Most travel books tell you how to travel like a tourist. Although there is nothing wrong with that, as part of the Greater Than a Tourist series, this book will give you travel tips from someone who has lived at your next travel destination.

   In these pages, you will discover advice that will help you throughout your stay. This book will not tell you exact addresses or store hours but instead will give you excitement and knowledge from a local that you may not find in other smaller print travel books.

   Travel like a local. Slow down, stay in one place, and get to know the people and the culture. By the time you finish this book, you will be eager and prepared to travel to your next destination.

TABLE OF CONTENTS

13. GET SOME IVY LEAGUE SMARTS:
14. GO TO THE THEATRE
15. GO TO THE MOVIES
16. MUSIC
17. RADIO
18. WHAT TO READ
19. BUY A BOOK
20. FENWAY PARK
21. THE BOSTON GARDEN
22. COLLEGE SPORT
23. THE HEAD OF THE CHARLES
24. THE BOSTON MARATHON
25. SOWA OPEN MARKET
26. EAT DIM SUM
27. EAT ICE CREAM
(ALL YEAR ROUND)
28. EAT PIZZA
29. THE LAWN ON D
30. GO CANDLEPIN BOWLING
31. BUY SOME ART
32. THE BOSTON HARBOR ISLANDS
33. THE ARNOLD ARBORETUM
34. TAKE A WALK DOWN OLD TORY ROW
35. ROSE KENNEDY GREENWAY
36. HARVARD UNIVERSTIY
37. JAMAICA PLAIN

\>TOURIST

DEDICATION

This book is dedicated to my parents, who brought me into this world along the banks of the Charles River and opened up so many doors to Boston's rich world of learning, culture, and science.

>TOURIST

ABOUT THE AUTHOR

Alexander Dunn was born and raised in Cambridge, Massachusetts. He has worked, lived, and played in Boston all his life. He holds a B.A. in creative writing and an M.Ed. in museum education. His work has always been guided by a sense of place (the complex and often subtle connections between landscape and people). He has worked for numerous Massachusetts based non-profits as a teacher, natural history guide, and museum professional. As of 2018 he is completing his first book and working as a science communications specialist. He likes to navigate the city by bicycle and will forever feel blessed for witnessing not one but three Red Sox Championships. He is proud to call Boston home.

>TOURIST

HOW TO USE THIS BOOK

The Greater Than a Tourist book series was written by someone who has lived in an area for over three months. The goal of this book is to help travelers either dream or experience different locations by providing opinions from a local. The author has made suggestions based on their own experiences. Please do your own research before traveling to the area in case the suggested places are unavailable.

>TOURIST

FROM THE PUBLISHER

Traveling can be one of the most important parts of a person's life. The anticipation and memories that you have are some of the best. As a publisher of the Greater Than a Tourist book series, as well as the popular 50 Things to Know book series, we strive to help you learn about new places, spark your imagination, and inspire you. Wherever you are and whatever you do I wish you safe, fun, and inspiring travel.

Lisa Rusczyk Ed. D.
CZYK Publishing

>TOURIST

OUR STORY

Traveling is a passion of the "Greater than a Tourist" series creator. Lisa studied abroad in college, and for their honeymoon Lisa and her husband toured Europe. During her travels to Malta, an older man tried to give her some advice based on his own experience living on the island since he was a young boy. She was not sure if she should talk to the stranger but was interested in his advice. When traveling to some places she was wary to talk to locals because she was afraid that they weren't being genuine. Through her travels, Lisa learned how much locals had to share with tourists. Lisa created the "Greater Than a Tourist" book series to help connect people with locals. A topic that locals are very passionate about sharing.

>TOURIST

WELCOME TO
> TOURIST

>TOURIST

INTRODUCTION

For Boston's not a capital,
And Boston's not a place;
Rather I feel that Boston is
The perfect state of grace.

From "Boston Is Like No Other Place in the World,
Only More So," by E. B. White

The 50 Tips included in this guide are ideas for things to do in Boston and the immediate surrounding towns of Cambridge, Somerville, Brookline, and Chelsea, as well as a few locations outside of the city that are easily accessible via public transit or a short drive. All of these experiences are indicative of Boston's culture and represent the sort of things I do with my friends and family when they visit. Some tips on this list will show up in Trip Advisor or mainstream travel guides, but more likely they are the kind of experiences that have authenticity, are unique to Boston, and represent the things I love to do as a local.

>TOURIST

1. BOSTON: A LAY OF THE LAND

Boston sits on the land once known as Shawmut and is home to the people of the Wampanoag Nation. European settlers first arrived in Massachusetts in 1620, famously landing at Plymouth Rock (not included in this book because it really is just a rock in a hole). The city arose where three rivers meet the ocean in the deep water Boston Harbor. The harbor is protected with islands that provide security from storms and were once the site for military defense. The land around the city held good timber and arable, though rocky soil. The British made themselves at home and those place names that don't come from a Native language are distinctly British, often with a "New" added on for good measure. In the 1770's Boston and the surrounding towns of Cambridge, Lexington and Concord were hotbeds for civil unrest and the area still holds deep ties to the American Revolution, early American Government and politics. Boston was home to Ben Franklin, Josiah Quincy, and yes, George Washington did sleep here. In more recent decades Boston is known for its ties to the Kennedys, John Kerry, and Mitt Romney.

In the 19th and early 20th centuries, Boston was known as a city of old money Brahmins, a sentiment captured in the often quoted line: "And this is good old Boston, The home of the bean and the cod, Where the Lowells talk to the Cabots, And the Cabots talk only to God." (John Collins Bossidy). While an old money legacy does remain, today's Boston is a city with a deep regional identity that is constantly evolving with the arrival of new immigrants, new money, and new development. It is a city where wealth, innovation, a strong working class, and academia mingle together to form a tough but affable stew.

As a city, Boston proper encompasses the neighborhoods of East Boston, Charlestown, North End, Financial District, Fort Point, Seaport, Back Bay, Fenway, South End, Allston, Brighton, South Boston, Financial District, Dorchester, Roxbury, West Roxbury, Jamaica Plain, Hyde Park, Mattapan, and Roslindale as well as numerous squares and centers within these neighborhoods.

The city is not huge with a population of around 670,000. The urban core of "Greater Boston" includes parts of neighboring cities Cambridge, Somerville, Everett, Chelsea, Brookline, Newtown, and Quincy. This urban center is easily accessed by the MBTA subway system known as "the T" and often, you won't know when you've left Boston and entered one of these neighboring towns. When people talk about "Greater Boston," they are including the towns surrounding Interstate 95 and some 4.7 million people (2017). Most of these towns are a mix of residential and suburban neighborhoods with a typically American mix of light industry, office parks, malls, town center, a city hall, library, and main street. While many are charming and distinct, they are often not easily accessible by public transit from downtown Boston and so do not appear in this guide.

2. BOSTON ACCENT

First things first, just don't do it. No "wicked pissah," "lobstah" or "pawk your cah in Havad yaad" nonsense. The Boston accent has been butchered and commercialized by movies and television for a long time. Real New England accents are numerous and varied. For more on this, watch Seth Meyer's fake movie trailer "Boston Accent." Translations to some of the colloquial phrases include: "bubbler" is a water fountain; "all set" means you don't need anything else; sports teams are the "Sox, Pats, B's and C's or Celts." A "frappe" is a milkshake, a "tonic" is a soda, and "regular" coffee comes with cream and sugar; "extra-extra" is basically a cup of cream and sugar with a splash of coffee on top. "Steamers" are clams, a "scorpion bowl" is a fruity, alcoholic punch served in a ceramic bowl for sharing. "Steak tips" are delicious, order them, and; you can buy your beer and wine from the "packie" or package store. Enjoy, but please don't try and imitate.

3. LOGAN AIRPORT

Boston's international airport is located in East Boston, just across the water from Downtown. Even though Logan is in the city proper, getting to and from the airport can be a chore. By car or taxi, you will be at the mercy of the traffic gods. Typical commuter hours are always bad. If you're coming or going between 7-9am or 4-6pm on a weekday, give yourself over an hour, even from downtown. It only takes a small fender bender to cause all kinds of backups. A better option than driving is public transit. You can get to the Airport stop on the Blue Line, where a free shuttle will get you to your terminal (A, B, C, D, or E). You can also take the Silver line from South Station. The Silver Line is a bus that primarily runs on proprietary lanes and tunnels. Either option will take between 30-45 mins. from downtown. A fun, though slightly pricier way to get there is by water taxi from Charlestown, the Courthouse or the downtown waterfront. A small boat will take you and your luggage across the harbor to the bus stop next to the Hyatt Regency hotel, where a free shuttle will take you to your gate.

4. WALK

Ralph Waldo Emerson famously said that Boston was "laid out by cows," and Bill Bryson wrote in "The Lost Continent" that "Boston's freeway system is insane. It was clearly designed by a person who had spent his childhood crashing toy trains." Either way, you get the point: Boston is known for its bad drivers, impossible parking, and a twisted city plan. The happy solution… walk. Boston is not a huge city, and at only 89 square miles it is smaller than Philadelphia (134), Chicago (234), New York City (304) and dwarfed by L.A. (503) or Houston (627). Though the city is larger than most people think, downtown is small and makes for great walking. If you get lost or tired, you can always find a nearby T stop (subway station) and today, rent a city bike, or of course, get a taxi or car service. Boston is fairly safe, and its history, living, working, eating and drinking spaces are interspersed, turning any stroll around Boston into an act of discovery and if you need to get away from the city crush for a bit there are numerous parks including the Common, Public Garden, Emerald Necklace, and Harbor Walk.

5. TAKE THE "T"

Boston's subway system is the oldest in the county and at times, it feels that way. It does, however, move millions of people around the city every year and typically runs smoothly. The T is a traditional subway with a combination of electric and gas powered trains and trolleys that operate both under and above ground. The system is divided into five lines, each represented by a color: red, blue, green, orange, and the silver line which is a bus system running mainly through allocated tunnels. The hub of the system is located at the square of stops formed by stations: Park Street, Downtown Crossing, State, and Government Center. Trains that are heading towards these stops are called "inbound" and trains going away, "outbound." Know that once you've passed through one of these stations your train can go from inbound to outbound. Trains running on the red, blue and orange lines are called by the last stop they are running towards, so check to see if you want to be headed towards Alewife or Ashmont/Braintree. The Greenline branches into a B, C, D, and E train after Copley. You pay a flat price to travel anywhere on the system, whether it's one stop or twenty. Payment is all through the ticket system known as the Charlie Card or a onetime Charlie ticket. You can make as many transfers as you want within the system but once you leave a station you will need to pay again to reenter. Even during winter storms, the T works well, although if you're staying out late you might need to take a taxi or car service home, as the last train is typically around 2 am. There is also a robust bus and commuter rail system, check online for maps and schedules.

6. DRIVING ME CRAZY

Boston is a famously bad driving city. The city is built around the meandering Charles River, filled with one-way streets, confusing highway interchanges, tunnels that go underwater, and populated with unsympathetic drivers. While there is plenty to do in Boston without a car, and you'll be fine without one, if you do rent or borrow a vehicle, here are some tips.

Like any metropolitan center, commuter traffic is bad coming into the city in the morning (7-9am) and again leaving the city in the afternoon (3pm-6pm). This is especially true on highways 2, 3, 90, 93, 95, and 128. The city has two ring-roads: 495 (further out) and 95 (which makes a small loop around downtown and goes to Newburyport MA, Portsmouth NH, Portland ME to the north and Providence, RI and New York City to the south). Rt. 90, known as the "Mass Pike," is a toll road that goes due west from the city towards Worcester, MA and Albany, NY. Rt. 2 will take you northwest, towards Lexington and Concord, MA. Rt. 3 runs southeast along the coast and connects to Plymouth and Cape Cod. 93 is known as the "Central Artery" or the "Southeast Expressway" and travels from central NH and goes right through the heart of downtown. Once elevated, 93 now travels through the infamous "Big Dig" tunnels. In the city, there are two arterial highways that follow either side of the Charles River. Memorial "Mem" Drive (Rt. 3) on the Cambridge Side and Storrow Drive on the Boston side. Most of the important in town streets have nicknames including: "Mass Ave" (Massachusetts Avenue), "Com Ave" (Commonwealth Avenue), "Dot Ave" (Dorchester Avenue), "The Pike" (Massachusetts Turnpike/Rt.

90), and anything "across the River" means Cambridge. Good luck!

7. VISIT THE BOSTON PUBLIC LIBRARY

No other building in Boston is more of a temple to the city than the Boston Public Library known as the "BPL." The library is located at Copley Square. It faces Trinity Church, sits under the shadow of the all-glass Prudential Center, and faces the finish line to the Boston Marathon on Boylston Street. It's as if all things lead to the BPL. The library itself is housed in two adjacent buildings, the older, McKimm Building, opened in 1854, and the 1972 extension. When the Boston Public library opened, it was the first public library in the country and the McKimm building is on the National Historic Register and considered one of the best examples of Beaux-Arts architecture in the country. Lavish, barrel arched ceilings, alfresco murals, carved columns and wood furniture make the space feel both grand and comfortable. View the John Singer Sargent Murals located on the 3rd floor, stop by the Norman B. Leventhal Map Center to see rotating exhibits from the permanent collection, browse a newspaper or read a book in the grand Bates

Hall. Bring your electronics and use the free wi-fi. In the new wing, or watch a live broadcast of National Public Radio's Boston affiliate WGBH as they record live (some weekdays) in the News Café. On warm days, the courtyard within the McKim Building is open to the public, and is an oasis from the grind of the city that surrounds you on all sides.

8. WALK AROUND THE BACK BAY

Between Mass Ave and the Common are several blocks of lovely streets lit by gas lamps, known as Back Bay, lined with the brick and brownstone dwellings of Victorian Boston. Newbury Street is the ritzy shopping zone, tree-lined Comm Ave. has a pedestrian path in the middle. Start at the Public Garden and walk down Comm Ave. Cut down Exeter Street to Boylston Street and have a drink at the Lenox Hotel bar or the Oak Room in the Fairmont Copley Plaza. Note that cross streets running between the river and downtown are alphabetical from (A)rlington to (H)ereford.

9. GET A BIRD'S EYE VIEW OF THE CITY

There are several places around Boston to get a great aerial view. From natural, historical to plush, here are a few of my favorites. Located on the 52nd floor of the Prudential Center, Top of the Hub, is a restaurant, bar, and observatory with pay-for-the-view priced drinks and food. Bunker Hill Monument in Charlestown is the 221' tall, granite obelisk built to commemorate the 1775 Battle of Bunker Hill. Climb to the top for some great views. Check the National Park Service webpage for hours of operation. For the outdoorsy, climb to the peak of Great Blue Hill located in the Blue Hills Reservation, in Milton. Make sure to check the state Department of Conservation and Recreation website for a map and list of ranger led walks and talks. Climb to the top of Washington Tower, the "castle looking thing" at the center of Mount Auburn Cemetery in Cambridge. The tower is open seasonally, though the view from the base is pretty great too, and accessible year round during regular cemetery hours.

10. EXPLORE THE EMERALD NECKLACE

Designed by the landscape architect, Fredrick Law Olmstead, the Emerald Necklace is the ribbon of parks, paths, and water that lace through the city from Jamaica Pond to the Public Garden. This green infrastructure was built to serve two purposes. First, it was an ingenious way to drain the smelly, sewage choked waters of the Back Bay, into the Charles River. Second, it created a path for then Victorians to go out for their afternoon amble and to socialize. Today the Emerald Necklace is protected by a public-private partnership and offers green space for biking, jogging, sports, and quiet. A wonderful lunch spot are the Victory Gardens, located near Fenway Park. These relics of WWII represent small garden plots that are leased to residents to grow fruits, vegetables, and flowers.

11. VISIT THE MUSEUM OF FINE ARTS BOSTON (MFA)

A world class museum with an encyclopedic collection from ancient Egypt to contemporary art. Highlights of the MFA include the Paul Revere silver, a turn of the century American portrait collection with works by Copley, Sargent, and Eakins, and a stellar impressionist collection. The new wing houses American arts from the 17th-20th century in tight, yet glass-walled rooms. Intermixing decorative arts like furniture, jewelry and model ships with portraits and landscapes, the effect is an immersive time capsule of America as recorded by the arts. Some of the hidden highlights inside the museum include the Egyptian mummies, the giant seated Buddha, and the musical instruments room. Check out the MFA online calendar for both their film series and their Late Nites series, which includes live music, cash bar and other non-traditional museum experiences.

12. ISABELLA STEWART GARDNER MUSEUM

This private collection is housed in the home of its patron and namesake, Isabella Stewart Gardner and represents an incredible collection of art and antiquities collected over one woman's lifetime. The museum is housed in Gardner's home, complete with garden courtyard and glass roof. I like to go on a rainy day when the glass roof pings with the sounds of rain and the stone and wood rooms become even darker and moodier. Check the museum's online event calendar for late night events, concerts series and music in the courtyard.

13. GET SOME IVY LEAGUE SMARTS:

Boston and Cambridge are home to over thirty colleges and universities. Today, most have sprawling, decentralized campuses with limited public access and a lot of security. A lot of visitors take a campus tour or just wander around campus, but if you want a glimpse into college life, check out the online events and public lectures listings for each school. Often these talks are given by the best in the field and held in the school's premiere lecture halls, theatres, or auditoriums. While you may stumble into some actual rocket science at MIT, and some of the physics may go over your head, it is a great chance to see inside university life. Check Berklee College of Music for concerts; ArtsEmerson for a listing of theatre and lectures at Emerson College; Harvard's, Mahindra Humanities Center series; or the Kennedy School's, Institute of Politics. The Harvard Museum of Natural History also holds frequent public lectures, and keep your eyes peeled for anything held at Sanders Theatre, which is an incredible venue. MIT's Media Lab, is host to "events, conferences, talks, and hackathons." It is also the source of a lot of cool robots and AI. Also at MIT is the List Visual Arts Center with many fascinating programs. Check the event pages for Boston University, Boston College, Northeastern, Simmons, Tufts, MassArt, UMass Boston, and the list goes on.

14. GO TO THE THEATRE

Enjoy music, dance or theatre in one of the city's premier venues. While you may think you don't love opera, symphony or theatre, just being in one of these spaces is enough to change your mind. Faded velvet, ornate paneling, balconies, and mezzanines, these venues have all the trappings of the heyday of society life. Tickets can vary in price, but last-minute seats and online deals are out there. The Boston Opera House is home to both the Boston Ballet, as well as numerous traveling operas. Symphony Hall is home to both the Boston Symphony Orchestra (BSO) as well as the Boston Pops, known for their cinematic music. The Emerson Colonial Theatre is a great place to see a play or splashy musical. Regardless of the event, Sander's Theatre at Memorial Hall in Cambridge is worth a visit. The wood paneling, chandelier, and octagonal walls give Sanders Theatre the reputation of actually being a character in the performance. Check the Office of the Arts at Harvard for upcoming event listings.

15. GO TO THE MOVIES

While most national movie theatres are now owned by the same corporation, Boston is home to a great collection of independent movie theatres, showing a range of films from foreign and art house to horrorand cult classics. The Brattle Theatre, located in Harvard Square, Cambridge is Boston's self-proclaimed "unofficial film school." The Brattle has been showing films since 1953, and with only one screen, you may not know the title of what you're about to see, but most likely you will come out moved by the experience. Eat dinner at the adjacent Alden and Harlow. The Harvard Film Archive, located near Harvard Yard in Cambridge, shows some really weird stuff like art house and experimental films. Coolidge Corner is another Boston institution, famous for their real buttered popcorn, movie marathons, lectures and After Midnight series showing all kinds of cult and horror classics. For many years the Coolidge has also run an outdoor, summer movie series on the Rose Kennedy Greenway. Kendal Square Cinema is the most mainstream theatre on this list and typically shows the more recent critically acclaimed and Oscar nominated titles, all from comfy seats. The Somerville Theatre, in Davis Square, Somerville, and the Capitol Theatre in Arlington both show new releases in a notably classic setting and are located within easy reach of some good restaurants. Bring a blanket and a picnic and enjoy a free, outdoor film with Movies at the Hatchshell, showing family classics on Friday nights during the summer.

16. MUSIC

Boston has some big music venues like The House of Blues, TD Garden, and the Blue Hills Bank Pavilion, but check out some of the smaller venues for a more local music scene: The Sinclair, or Middle East, both in Cambridge; the Paradise Rock Club, in Allston; or

Wally's Jazz Café, in Roxbury. There are also some great music events around the city, including Jazz at the Fort in Roxbury's Highland Park; and Boston Calling, a multi-day, multi-venue festival that brings big and indie names to the city, or slightly further afield the Lowell Folk Festival and the Newport (RI) Jazz Fest.

17. RADIO

Boston is well known as a college town, and the tight proximity of universities and colleges not only means cheap burritos and beer but also some great independent college radio stations. Listen to an ever changing mix of musical mash up from folk, and underground hip hop, to bluegrass, indie rock, mid-day jazz, live opera, or whatever else the DJ feels like putting on. Here is a brief list of college stations worth tuning into: 88.1 MIT; 88.9 Emerson; 89.7 National Public Radio, news, talk and commentary; 90.3 Boston College; 90.9 Boston University / NPR; 91.5 Tufts; 91.9 UMass Boston – Folk; 95.3 Harvard which during reading periods hosts "orgies" and will play a single artist for hours, even days at a time. For live sports and endless commentary go to 850 AM for

Red Sox games and 98.5 FM for Celtics, Bruins, and Patriot games.

18. WHAT TO READ

Dozens of well-known authors and literary dignitaries have called Boston home. While visiting, you should read a book that is both entertaining, and has Boston at its center. Titles you to consider include: "The Dante Club," by Matthew Pearl which is a murder mystery set in civil war era Cambridge. Though fictional, it features the very real Henry Wadsworth Longfellow, Oliver Wendell Holmes and James Russell Lowell, and perfectly complements a stroll down Brattle St. in Cambridge. Before there was the movie, there was the book "Black Mass," by Gerald O'Neill. This incredible retelling of the weird and violently corrupt entanglement of Whitey Bulger's Winter Hill Gang the FBI, and Boston police is a page turner. "The Art Forger," by B.A. Shapiro is a fictional account of a painter who gets entwined in a very real, and still unsolved 1990 art heist at the Gardner Museum. Titles in the Spenser detective series by Robert B. Parker are all set in modern day Boston, as well as many works by Dennis Lehane including "Gone Baby Gone, Moonlit Mile or Mystic River" while Lehane's "The Given Day" is set in 1919 Boston. Additional Boston titles include: "The Proper Bostonians," by Cleveland Amory "The

Bostonians," by Henry James; and "Run," by Ann
Patchett;

19. BUY A BOOK

Across the country, Amazon, Barnes and Nobles, and
e-readers have all but killed the local, independent
bookstore. Luckily, Boston is still home to some great
ones. The most iconic bookseller in the city is the
Brattle Book Shop located near Downtown Crossing.
It was established in 1825 and remains a joy for
browsing used and rare books as well as inexpensive
paperbacks. While Harvard Square, Cambridge was
once home to a dozen bookshops, it still retains a few
greats. Don't confuse the Harvard Book Store with
the Harvard Coop. The Harvard Bookstore has been a
purveyor of new books since 1932. High shelves,
knowledgeable staff, and a bargain basement, it
remains a bustling Cambridge staple. The Harvard
Coop (pronounced like a chicken coop) is the place to
buy shirts, calendars, and textbooks, but know that
while it has a great collection of titles, it is now
owned and operated by Barnes and Nobles. Located
just around the corner from the Harvard Book Store,
is the Grolier Poetry Bookshop. It may not be the
only one in the world but it has to be one of the few.

Operating since 1927, and selling only poetry, this place is a gem and worth a stop. The Lucy Parsons Center in Jamaica Plain is a self-described "independent, non-profit, radical bookstore and community space" and is "run collectively by our volunteers—no bosses, no pay." True to its mission, this is the place to find lesser known and radical titles, zines, and materials on organizing for change. The Brookline Booksmith has a huge selection of new and used books and is a great place to spend a lazy afternoon browsing.

20. FENWAY PARK

Boston loves it sports, and there is no better place in the city to witness this love like Fenway Park, home to the Boston Red Sox. As one of the oldest remaining parks in the country, Fenway has become hallowed ground for baseball aficionados and retains its dingy, underground bathrooms, and dark corridors veneered in hot dogs, spilled beer and peanut shells. Fans are loyal, involved and increasingly less bitter than they were before 2004 when an 86-year drought was finally ended with a World Series championship. If you go to a game you'll see people listening to the radio broadcast, filling in a box score, and over hear grey-haired grannies comparing bullpen stats. Success, however, has brought riches, and as one of the smallest stadiums in the MLB, tickets can be hard to get. If the sox are in town, try online Stubhub.com or Ebay (though there is the risk of getting a fake, so read seller reviews carefully). If you do go down to the ballpark on game day, there will be guys asking about tickets. Buying a scalped ticket is technically illegal, but it happens. What if you can't get a ticket? Personally, I would never pay for a tour of the stadium but if you're a baseball nut and the Sox are out of town, it is an option. If you can't get a ticket, I'd recommend watching the game from a local bar along Lansdowne or Comm Ave. Towards the late innings, they open up the gated area around Yawkey Way (a street scheduled for a name change) and the Italian sausages sell two for one. You'll get all the tough love, cursing and spilled beer you want and get a sense of Red Sox nation in person. Try the Bleacher Bar (for an actual view of the game), or the Cask and Flaggin for some yelling at the TV.

21. THE BOSTON GARDEN

The historic Boston Garden was razed in the late 90s and replaced by the TD Garden. Located above North Station with access to the orange, green and commuter rail lines, it is home to both the Celtics (NBA basketball) who play from October to June and the Bruins (NHL hockey) who play from October to May. Tickets are usually available online or at the box office. Make sure to bask in the banners that hang from the rafters and represent conference and championships, as well as retired players' numbers marking some of the many eras of both the green and black and gold.

22. COLLEGE SPORT

With all the area colleges, amateur sports are alive and well in Boston. The highlights of college sports in Boston are the Bean Pot, and the Harvard Yale Game. The Bean Pot is a hockey tournament featuring local hockey powerhouses: Harvard, Boston College, Northeastern, and Boston University. Teams are pitted against each other during the first two weekends in February. The Harvard vs Yale football game is unabashedly known as "The Game," and typically occurs in November. If either of these events aren't going on, get a ticket for any college football, basketball, hockey, track, lacrosse, swimming, soccer or rugby match. It's a chance to see up and coming talent at an affordable price and get an inside look at college life in the city.

23. THE HEAD OF THE CHARLES

During the 3rd weekend in October, the Head of the Charles brings rowers from around the world to this historic regatta. Boats with a crew of one to eight, pull oars in different classes and navigate the twisty Charles River. The race course goes from the Pierce Boathouse at MIT to just beyond the Eliot Bridge, and spectators line the banks of the Charles River on both the Cambridge and Boston sides, as well as the bridges to watch racing shells go by. Rowers from high schools, colleges, and clubs representing all ages pull oars and navigate sharp turns in long, thin racing shells. It's a glimpse into a tradition that goes back to old Oxford and smacks of preppies in sweater vests and beanies. The event draws some 400,000 spectators to watch the roughly 10,000 athletes and is basically a big party. Outsiders are welcome. Tip: don't bring a car anywhere near the river that weekend, as many roads are closed and parking, already at a premium will be even rarer. Instead walk from the Harvard T stop or better yet, rent bikes and take Memorial Drive, which is closed to vehicle traffic along much of the route.

24. THE BOSTON MARATHON

The third Monday of April is Patriots' Day, a holiday commemorating the battles at Lexington and Concord. The day is not only marked with school and bank closures, a Red Sox day game, but also as "Marathon Monday." The Boston Marathon is the oldest marathon in the country and has been run since 1897. Today the event brings some 30,000 runners and a whole lot of supporters to the city. While hotels and flights are at a premium, it's basically a big party and a fun time to be in town. Supporters line both sides of the entire 28.5 miles from the starting line in Hopkinton to the finish line at Copley Square in Boston, and post-race burgers and beers are the norms. If you want to run the iconic race, you'll either need a previous marathon time of close to 3:30 (varying by age and gender) or you'll have to join a charity team to raise money for both the entry fee and a donation. For the less ambitious, pack a picnic, find a spot and cheer on the elite marathoners, then wave after wave of suffering, yet happy runners.

25. SOWA OPEN MARKET

Spend a lazy Sunday afternoon at the South of Washington, SOWA Open Market running from May to October, from 10 am-4 pm. Located in the SoWa Art + Design District along Harrison Ave. between Thayer Street and Paul Sullivan Way in the South End, this market is home to both temporary and permanent vendors selling everything from produce to art. During the outdoor Sunday market, food trucks circle up and sell street eats to a hip crowd. Even on other days, there are plenty of restaurants and galleries, as well as the Vintage Market.

26. EAT DIM SUM

Boston has a historic, if small China Town, located near South Station, with a traditional mix of produce markets, stores, and restaurants. One highlight is Sunday dim-sum. Lines are common, but worth the wait for a belly full of steamed buns, dumplings, seared vegetables and seafood. Popular locales include Empire Garden, located in a 113-year-old theater; Hei La Moon; Chau Chow City; China Pearl; Bubor Cha Cha; Winsor Dim Sum Café; and the Great Taste Bakery & Restaurant.

27. EAT ICE CREAM (ALL YEAR ROUND)

Though Massachusetts has fallen to 4th in U.S. ice cream consumption per capita it is still a pastime we take seriously, and there are a lot of great places to get a cone, even in the winter. Made on the premises, Toscanini's Ice Cream, in East Cambridge has both classic and a few bizarre flavors; J.P. Licks now operates multiple locations, but the original in Jamaica Plain is worth a visit; and Christina's in Inman Square, Somerville a longtime favorite. For extra points, try ordering a "frappe" in winter.

28. EAT PIZZA

Yes, Boston has a chip on its shoulder about New York, its cooler, prettier, richer older sister. And yes, New York has some great pizza but let it be known that Boston can hold its own. Thin slices from

Boston's own Uppercrust or Otto's from Portland, Maine can be found at multiple locations around the city. For a more downhome pie try Santarpios, located in East Boston or Pizzeria Regina, in the North End. Newcomers like Area4, Kendall Square, Cambridge, have been getting a lot of good press. But for the best slice, and as a sentimentalist, I have to give the honor to my childhood spot, Armando's Pizza & Subs located in Cambridge. This family run, take-out spot only has a few tables but has been fueling youth soccer players, family movie nights, and Harvard astrophysicists, for decades.

29. THE LAWN ON D

Part event space, part bar, part playground for grownups, the Lawn on D is one of those quirky outcomes of soaring property values, new development and an eye for livable communities. Started in 2015, it describes itself as an "outdoor interactive space and experimental event landscape." The Lawn is complete with illuminated swings, installation art, a performance stage (check schedule for events), free lawn games, lounge chairs, and that rare green commodity in the city… grass. It has quickly become a popular summertime hangout, so bring a picnic and unplug or bring the laptop and use the free wi-fi.

30. GO CANDLEPIN BOWLING

This unique New England sport is played on a regular bowling alley with bocce sized balls. The game differs from regular ten-pin bowling in several ways. You get three balls to try and knock down ten, slender wood pins. In between each ball the downed pins are not cleared allowing you to use the "dead wood" to spin, knock and send standing pins over. Since the balls are much lighter than tenpin, it seems like it should be easier, but candlepin is deceptively hard. Similarities to traditional bowling include renting smelly shoes, drinking beer, and eating pizza. There are also league nights, competitions and whole associations devoted to the sport. Finding candlepin is becoming increasingly hard, as bowling alleys are closing to the pressure of rising property values and new development. A few holdouts still exist. For the true experience check out: Sacco's Bowl Haven, in Davis Square, Somerville or South Boston Candlepin.

31. BUY SOME ART

The Mass Art Made Sale is the Massachusetts College of Art's student art sale. Mass Art, located in the Fenway, is the country's only public art college, and this reoccurring sale not only supports struggling student artists but also showcases the impressive work of artists moving towards the top of their game. Who knows, someday they may be famous! Also, check out Artists for Humanity located in the South End, an organization that supports creative and entrepreneurial teens through the sale of their art.

32. THE BOSTON HARBOR ISLANDS

Boston is a city on the sea, a port town known for its seafood and maritime history. But it's easy to take a trip to Boston and never really get a real view of the water. The best way to get a deep breath of salt air from Downtown is by taking the ferry to one of the Boston Harbor Islands. Once home forts, prisons, and military installations today the Harbor Islands are now open to the public, operated by the National Parks, and accessible by public ferry. The boat ride itself is part of the fun, running from mid-May to early October (check online for a schedule) or visit the ticket booth located on Long Wharf by the Boston Marriot. The ferries are for foot passengers only and leave every few hours. Tickets are reasonably priced, as you only pay to go out, inter-island trips and returns are included. From Long Wharf you can visit Georges, Spectacle and Peddocks Islands or take a longer trip to Boston Light, which is a tiny rock with a lighthouse located at the mouth of Boston Harbor. Pack a lunch and blanket and plan to spend the day. Once on the island, explore the grassy slopes, old forts, or just gaze back at the city. If you plan early (or get lucky) you can book a campsite and spend a night or two.

33. THE ARNOLD ARBORETUM

Get a breath of fresh air at the Arnold Arboretum. This 280-acre parcel of land is home to a "living collection" of plants, trees, and shrubs owned and operated by Harvard University. Car free trails lace through the Arboretum, and while April-May are the most popular times to see the blooming lilacs, bulbs, and fruit trees, there is no bad time to visit. Biking and picnicking are welcomed, and as an arboretum,

most of the plants and trees are labeled with their
names in both Latin and English. Walk up Peter's Hill
for some great views of downtown Boston. The
Arboretum is accessible from the Forest Hills T stop
on the Orange Line or via bike or foot from the
Southwest Corridor bike trail and sits between the
busy Boston neighborhoods of Roslindale, Jamaica
Plain and Roxbury. Visit the website to customize
your own plant tour, view a map and check for
upcoming events, guided walks, or lectures.

34. TAKE A WALK DOWN OLD TORY ROW

Head West from Harvard Square in Cambridge
along Brattle Street and you'll meander through some
of the historic homes of the "Tories," who were loyal
to the Queen. You'll pass landmarks like the
Longfellow House - Washington's Headquarters
National Historic Site, operated by the National Park
Service and former home of Henry Wadsworth
Longfellow. Cross the busy Rt. 3 and Brattle Street
will bring you out near the entrance to Mount Auburn
Cemetery. Known as America's first garden
cemetery, this is not a morbid place, but filled with

trees, flowers, and flowing hills. It's the resting place for many of Boston's wealthy elites, academics, literary and artistic thinkers. Pick up a map at the gatehouse and make your way to the Washington Tower (open spring-fall) for an incredible view of the whole city and region. As this is an active cemetery, leave the pets, bikes, running shoes and picnic at home, walk with respect and enjoy.

35. ROSE KENNEDY GREENWAY

The Rose Kennedy Greenway is the green space and chain of parks that run along the downtown waterfront. Built in the footprint of the Central Artery, an elevated section of highway 95 that now runs underground, thanks to the infamous Big Dig (three decades and $24 billion later). The Rose Kennedy Greenway starts near Faneuil Hall and the North End and curves around the Shawmut Peninsula to Fort Point. Walk in either direction and be assured that there is Italian food at one end in the North End and James Hook lobster company at the other. Public art, food trucks, lawn games, outdoor movies, and sunbathing occur regularly during warm weather. Stop at the Boston Public Market, a year-round, indoor farmers market, and pick up a picnic of local bread, cheese, meats, produce, chocolate, coffee, beer and wine. Visitors with kids should take a ride on the carousel with hand-carved, native New England animals including a lobster and Peregrine Falcon.

36. HARVARD UNIVERSTIY

Everyone walks through Harvard Yard to rub John Harvard's shoe, but to see a more interesting side of the university, head out of Harvard Yard onto Quincy Street where you'll find the Harvard Art Museums. Home to ancient, European and modern art, the entire collection is housed in a newly renovated building. From there, walk to the Carpenter Center for Visual Arts, housed in the only North American building designed by Swiss architect, Le Corbusie. While the Carpenter Center houses active classrooms and studios, there is a public gallery, film archive sweeping, public causeway that are all open to the public. Walk to the massive Memorial Hall and follow Oxford Street north. Look for the unassuming Peabody Museum of Anthropology and Natural History Museum both located at the far end of the lawn. Inside you'll find the famous glass flower exhibit, as well as the hall of mammals, an old school collection of mounted animals specimens and objects of cultural heritage from around the world. Behind the museums on the Biology Quad is the famous brass Rhino and the Diquís Ball, a 4,800lbs stone sphere that sits outside the Tozzer Library on Divinity Street. For Harvard souvenirs, don't waste your money on mugs or key chains. Instead, visit Bob Slates Stationary for Harvard branded notebooks, pens, and calendars.

37. JAMAICA PLAIN

Known locally as "JP" this neighborhood has a great concentration of restaurants, cafes, and bakeries, as well as music, vintage, and art stores. Walk the tightly packed, though stretched out, urban core of the neighborhood along Centre Street, or escape to the natural namesake, Jamaica Pond. The neighborhood has a mix of Cuban and Salvadorian restaurants, along with Irish bars, the Sam Adams Brewery, and Saturday farmer's market (May – Nov). Check out longtime icons like Tres Gatos for wine, tapas, books, and music; JP Licks for ice cream, and 40 South Street for vintage clothing. The area can be reached on the Orange Line, Jackson Square stop.

38. NORTH END

Boston's historic Italian neighborhood, the North End has retained some of its cultural identity, despite increases in city-wide housing prices and constant development. The heart of the north end is packed along Hanover and Salem Streets, between Prince and Cross. Famous for food, espresso, and pastries, you can't go wrong eating in the North End. Spend a half hour walking around and checking out menus. Don't judge a place on its size or linens, as simple can be great (Giacomo's, Galleria Umberto, The Daily Catch), and tiny can be wildly popular (Neptune Oyster). For dessert, pass on the hype of the Modern vs. Mike's Pastry battle, and hit up Bova's Bakery (open 24 hours). You can get to the North End from the North Station, Haymarket, or Aquarium T stops or simply walk over from the Rose Kennedy Greenway from Downtown.

39. INMAN SQUARE

Located at the intersection of Cambridge, Prospect, Beacon, and Hampshire streets in Somerville, Inman Square is not on the T but is a thriving neighborhood worth a visit for dinner or a drink. Hihglights include: Christina's ice cream; Punjab Dhaba, inexpensive Indian food served hot and fast on metal trays; Moonas or Oleana for top notch Middle Eastern cuisine; the Midwest Grille for gaucho style Brazilian steak; or Restaurant Casa Portugal representing the longtime Portuguese, Brazilian, and Cape Verdean communities living in the area. For a drink, try Trina's Starlite Lounge, The Druid, Parlor, or slightly further down, Lord Hobo for a huge beer selection.

40. DAVIS SQUARE

Home to Tufts University and located just on the Cambridge/Somerville line, Davis Square is a tightly packed neighborhood with some great venues for eating, drinking, hearing music or seeing a show. Longtime eateries include Rosebud Café, Redbones BBQ, Mikes, or Anna's Taqueria. Or try a more recent addition like Saloon, Foundery on Elm, or Meju Korean Kitchen. For activities visit the Museum of Bad Art, Sacco's Bowl Haven, or the Somerville Theatre for a movie. Check out the Porch Fest website for dates and venues for concerts held right on people's porches and if you're around in October, find the date for Honk, the "activist band festival," when marching bands from across the country convene in Davis Square for a parade and empowerment to the people. Accessible from the redline, Davis T stop.

41. CENTRAL SQUARE

Central Square represents the heart of Cambridge. Running along Mass Ave from the split with Main Street to a few blocks past Prospect Street. This long neighborhood is great to wander for dinner, coffee, a drink or some shopping. A trio of well-worn bars includes the Plough and Stars, the People's Republik, The Field, and the Can-Tab Lounge, which all cater to locals, barflies, college students, musicians, Red Sox fans, and street philosophers. A more recent crop of good eating and drinking spots include Green Street Grille, Little Donkey, Central Kitchen, Cuchi-Cuchi, and Cragie on Main, Miracle of Science and long time, late night eatery, Moody's Falafel Palace. Live music can be found most nights at the Plough and Stars, the Middle East, Phoenix Landing, and Thelonious Monkfish (jazz), and the Middlesex Lounge (DJ). There is some eclectic shopping to be done in Central from Seven Stars new age bookstore, the Korean market chain H-Mart, Cambridge Bicycle,

MIT Bookstore, Hilton Tent City, Rodney's Bookstore, or the Artist and Craftsman Supply. There are numerous coffee spots, as well as healthy and veggie/vegan eateries. In September, the Cambridge Carnival takes place in Central Square, celebrating African and Caribbean culture and featuring music, food, and a parade. You can reach Central Square from the redline Central T stop or the #1 bus that runs from Harvard Square to Dudley Square along Mass Ave.

42. FORT POINT

Take any of the bridges (Seaport Blvd, Congress Street, or Summer Street) from South Station over the small Fort Point channel and you will be in the neighborhood of Fort Point. Formerly home to factories, many of the brick buildings have since been torn down to make way for large new developments. However, what does remain in this roughly three by six block area known as Fort Point, is a lively arts and business district with an overall feel for Boston's industrial heyday. Revolutionary history buffs will enjoy the Boston Tea Party Ships and Museum, a re-creation of the British boat that saw its cargo of tea dumped into the Boston harbor by colonial rebels, infamously dressed as Native Americans to hide their identities. This event is cited as one of the major triggers of the American Revolution. Past the tea party boat, you'll see the large Hood Milk Bottle which marks the entrance to the Boston Children's Museum, a great spot for kids aged 2-10 years old, though it often hosts evening events for adults as well. Enter into the canyons of brick, and you can find some great eating and drinking spots including Lucky's, Drink, City Tap House, and the Trillium Brewery (who are making some of the highest rated beer in the country). Fort Point is also known for its artists' studios, so check the Fort Point Arts Community website for a list of open studio tours that happen throughout the year.

43. SEAPORT

While Fort Point represents the old Boston, the surrounding neighborhood represents the new. The Seaport district is the area running along the harbor front, just north of Fort Point. Get there on the Silverline Bus. This area is home to some big buildings, including the Moakley Courthouse, Boston Convention Center, World Trade Center, and several large hotels and corporate offices. The numerous bars and restaurants are packed with tourists, but also fill up with local suits for after work drinks. Several of the bars have waterfront views or roof decks. Closer to downtown is the Barking Crab, serving basic fried seafood and cocktails in plastic cups. This place attracts happy hour lawyers and suits from the financial district. Further down Seaport Blvd. is Whiskey Priest with water views and a roof deck, and past this is an ever-changing list of high-end steak and seafood places, including one of many Legal Seafood. You pay for the view, so go for a sunset beer and cup of chowder but get dinner somewhere else. Further down Seaport Blvd. is the Harpoon Brewery, which offers tours and tastings but closes early. Cultural attractions include the Institute of Contemporary Art (ICA) which is located in a very cool building and home to some cutting edge, though often weird exhibits, definitely worth a visit. Bring a sandwich or coffee and sit on the large wood steps located on the water under the glass overhang of the ICA.

44. GET OUT OF TOWN

Boston's geography puts it within easy proximity to a lot of other great spots that can be reached by

plane, train or automobile. New York City is a 3-6
hour drive, pending traffic. Flights into LaGuardia
run about the same price as an Amtrak ticket, but
won't drop you in the city at Penn Station. The
Amtrak is the most comfortable trip, with the slightly
faster Acela or the slower, but more affordable
Regional, both leaving several times a day from
South Station. The cheapest way to NYC is on one of
the many buses that leave from South Station bus
terminal. Compare prices for the BoltBus, Peter Pan,
Greyhound, and Megabus. If you have a car, consider
making a trip to Northampton, MA a small college
town with a hippie vibe; Portsmouth, NH a slightly
touristy, harbor town with seafood and shopping; or
Portland, ME with a booming food and beer scene all
located within a few hours drive of Boston.

45. WALDEN POND

Located twenty minutes northwest of Boston in
Concord, Walden Pond is both a pilgrimage site for
environmentalists and writers as well as a popular
swimming hole. It is now a state park nestled into
adjacent conservation lands, making it a wonderful
place for a walk or contemplative sit. Famously home
to Henry David Thoreau, you can visit a reproduction

of his house as well as the original house site itself. Thoreau fans hoping for a tranquil moment are sometimes surprised to find the parking area full and the pond teeming with swimmers and sunbathers. If the main lot is full and you're up for a walk, park at Hapgood Wright Forest and walk over. Additionally, visit in the offseason or midweek, but on summer weekends, plan to get there early. While in Concord, make a day of transcendentalism and revolutionary history with a visit to the Old Manse, former home of Nathaniel and Sophia Hawthorne and Ralph Waldo Emerson; author's ridge at Sleepy Hollow Cemetery; Orchard House, home to Louisa May Alcott; and the Old North Bridge.

46. THE NORTH SHORE

For an easy day trip from Boston, take the Commuter Rail from North Station on the Rockport/Newburyport line and visit the north shore. The North Shore is a collection of seaside towns, including Salem, Manchester, Gloucester, Rockport, and Newburyport. Salem is known for its witches, and the month of October is one long black and orange themed party. The other eleven months of the year, it is a thriving little city located on the water.

With lots of good restaurants, breweries and non-witch related culture like the Peabody Essex Museum and the House of the Seven Gables. Manchester-by-the-Sea (yes that's it real name) is a tiny, up-scale town made popular by its easy access to Singing Beach. Further north the line splits, one running to Rockport, the other to Newburyport. The Rockport line takes you to Gloucester, one of the last surviving fishing towns in Massachusetts and is home to some great seafood, and some salty bars. Rockport is a bit more precious, a dry town but very walkable, with gift shop lined streets. Newburyport is the end of the other line, and a classic New England town, with narrow streets, brick buildings and views of the Merrimack River.

47. BEACHES

Whether you visit in summer or winter, know that Boston is located within 1.5 hours of some great beaches. Take into account that on hot summer days, the parking lots fill up fast and you'll spend a lot of time in traffic. So go during the week, get there early or go at the end of the day. In the off season beaches are empty with just a few hardy dog walkers, offering bleak, windy, but stunning views of the Atlantic.

Some of the most beloved beaches within a close shot of Boston include: Plum Island, Newburyport; Cranes Beach, Ipswich; Wingaersheek and Good Harbor both in Gloucester; Duxbury Beach, Duxbury; Horseneck, Westport; or slightly further Cape Cod National Seashore; Newport, RI; and Hampton Beach, NH.

48. TAKE THE HIGH-SPEED FERRY TO P-TOWN

If you look at the map of Massachusetts, you'll notice the Eastern part of the state juts out into the Atlantic Ocean like a curling arm. This 65-mile spit of land is known as Cape Cod, beginning at the Canal and ending at Race Point Light. "The Cape" is a varied landscape, home to some of Massachusetts's last remaining fishing fleets, lobstermen, and oyster beds, along with the state's best beaches. It is a major summertime tourist destination, and drive times from Boston to the tip of Provincetown can take anywhere from 2.5 to 4 hours, depending on traffic. The appeal is small towns, cedar shingle Cape houses, and miles of straight sand beaches. But now there is an easy and fun way to get to the cape in just 90 minutes. The Province Town Fast Ferry which is "the largest and fastest catamaran of its kind in North America" leaves from Downtown Boston and arrives in the heart of Provincetown just 90 minutes later. P-town is one of the Cape's most iconic destinations. It is a long time artist colony, gay cultural hub, and tourist destination, complete with narrow streets, lined with bars, gift shops, inns, and restaurants. P-Town is also home to the Cape Cod National Seashore, and is the start of several miles of bicycle trails that lace through dunes and pitch pine forest, as well as amazing views of the wide-open Atlantic Ocean. Make a reservation for both the boat and a place to stay before going.

49. WINTER IN THE CITY

Boston can have some long winters, and with its close proximity to Canada, it is no wonder that ice skating is alive and well in the city. When the nights get cold, go rent skates and take a twirl. Outdoor public ice skating can be found at: the Frog Pond on the Boston Common; Winterfest at Government Center; outside the Charles Hotel in Harvard Square Cambridge; the Kelly Outdoor Rink in Jamaica Plain; or at Community Ice Skating in Kendall Square, Cambridge. For some serious holiday lights, consider taking the Illuminations Tour, with the Somerville Arts Council. For holiday shopping, visit the Harvard Square Holiday Fair, Cambridge, open weekends in December leading up to Christmas. This pop-up craft fair is a great place to get your shopping done early.

50. JAYWALKING

Growing up in Boston, I never realized jaywalking was a thing. I assumed it was just how you cross the street. It wasn't until I traveled to other cities that I realized crossing without a "walk" sign or outside the crosswalk is illegal. In Boston, we walk as aggressively as we drive. When we see an opportunity – we take it. As a visitor, you should know that when people in front of you begin to cross the street, it does not mean it is legal or even safe to do so and you should check for yourself before you step off the curb. Jaywalking happens not only when the streets are empty, but also in the tiny spaces between speeding cars. So make sure you check both ways, use the crosswalk, or join the locals and enjoy the game of weaving through rushing traffic for yourself. Know that the term "jaywalking" doesn't refer to locals, but rather newcomers to the city, who used to be called "jays," and would stand in the

middle of the street, marveling at all the huge
buildings.

TOP REASONS TO BOOK THIS TRIP

Boston is the perfect size for a short or long vacation. Highlights are packed into one small harbor side city, and you can easily access history, culture, and great food on foot or public transit.

Boston retains a strong cultural identity. With deep roots into America's history, it is also a city doing the work of the future in medicine, technology, arts and engineering. On the subway, you'll sit between a descendent of the Mayflower and a newly arrived international medical student.

It's a city located equidistant from street hot dogs in New York City and seaside lobster rolls in Maine. It is the "Hub of the Universe."

>TOURIST

BONUS BOOK

50 THINGS TO KNOW ABOUT PACKING LIGHT FOR TRAVEL

Pack the Right Way Every Time

Author: Manidipa Bhattacharyya

>TOURIST

Edited by Melanie Howthorne

Introduction

He who would travel happily
must travel light.

-Antoine de Saint-Exupéry

Travel takes you to different places from seas and mountains to deserts and much more. In your travels you get to interact with different people and their cultures. You will, however, enjoy the sights and interact positively with these new people even more, if you are travelling light.

When you travel light your mind can be free from worry about your belongings. You do not have to spend precious vacation time waiting for your luggage to arrive after a long flight. There is be no chance of your bags going missing and the best part is that you need not pay a fee for checked baggage.

People who have mastered this art of packing light will root for you to take only one carry-on, wherever you go. However, many people can find it really hard to pack light. More so if you are travelling with children. Differentiating between "must have" and "just in case" items is the starting point. There will be ample shopping avenues at your destination which are just waiting to be explored.

This book will show you 'packing' in a new 'light' – pun intended – and help you to embrace light packing practices for all of your future travels.

Off to packing!

Dedication

I dedicate this book to all the travel buffs that I know, who have given me great insights into the contents of their backpacks.

About The Author

Manidipa Bhattacharyya is a creative writer and editor, with an education in English literature and Linguistics. After working in the IT industry for seven long years she decided to call it quits and follow her heart instead. Manidipa has been ghost writing, editing, proof reading and doing secondary research services for many story tellers and article writers for about three years. She stays in Kolkata, India with her husband and a busy two year old. In her own time Manidipa enjoys travelling, photography and writing flash fiction.

Manidipa believes in travelling light and never carries anything that she couldn't haul herself on a trip. However, travelling with her child changed the scenario. She seemed to carry the entire world with her for the baby on the first two trips. But good sense prevailed and she is again working her way to becoming a light traveler, this time with a kid.

The Right Travel Gear

1. Choose Your Travel Gear Carefully

While selecting your travel gear, pick items that are light weight, durable and most importantly, easy to carry. There are cases with wheels so you can drag them along – these are usually on the heavy side because of the trolley. Alternatively a backpack that you can carry comfortably on your back, or even a duffel bag that you can carry easily by hand or sling across your body are also great options. Whatever you choose, one thing to keep in mind is that the luggage itself should not weigh a ton, this will give you the flexibility to bring along one extra pair of shoes if you so desire.

2. Carry The Minimum Number Of Bags

Selecting light weight luggage is not everything. You need to restrict the number of bags you carry as well. One carry-on size bag is ideal for light travel. Most carriers allow one cabin baggage plus one purse, handbag or camera bag as long as it slides under the seat in front. So technically, you can carry two items of luggage without checking them in.

3. Pack One Extra Bag

Always pack one extra empty bag along with your essential items. This could be a very light weight duffel bag or even a sturdy tote bag which takes up minimal space. In the event that you end up buying a lot of souvenirs, you already have a handy bag to stuff all that into and do not have to spend time hunting for an appropriate bag.

I'm very strict with my packing and have everything in its right place. I never change a rule. I hardly use anything in the hotel room. I wheel my own wardrobe in and that's it.

Charlie Watts

Clothes & Accessories

4. Plan Ahead

Figure out in advance what you plan to do on your trip. That will help you to pick that one dress you need for the occasion. If you are going to attend a wedding then you have to carry formal wear. If not, you can ditch the gown for something lighter that will be comfortable during long walks or on the beach.

5. Wear That Jacket

Remember that wearing items will not add extra luggage for your air travel. So wear that bulky jacket that you plan to carry for your trip. This saves space and can also help keep you warm during the chilly flight.

6. Mix and Match

Carry clothes that can be interchangeably used to reinvent your look. Find one top that goes well with a couple of pairs of pants or skirts. Use tops, shirts and jackets wisely along with other accessories like a scarf or a stole to create a new look.

7. Choose Your Fabric Wisely

Stuffing clothes in cramped bags definitely takes its toll which results in wrinkles. It is best to carry wrinkle free, synthetic clothes or merino tops. This will eliminate the need for that small iron you usually bring along.

8. Ditch Clothes Pack Underwear

Pack more underwear and socks. These are the things that will give you a fresh feel even if you do not get a chance to wear fresh clothes. Moreover these are easy to wash and can be dried inside the hotel room itself.

9. Choose Dark Over Light

While picking your clothes choose dark coloured ones. They are easy to colour coordinate and can last longer before needing a wash. Accidental food spills and dirt from the road are less visible on darker clothes.

10. Wear Your Jeans

Take only one pair of Jeans with you, which you should wear on the flight. Remember to pick a pair that can be worn for sightseeing trips and is equally eloquent for dinner. You can add variety by adding light weight cargoes and chinos.

11. Carry Smart Accessories

The right accessory can give you a fresh look even with the same old dress. An intelligent neck-piece, a couple of bright scarves, stoles or a sarong can be used in a number of ways to add variety to your clothing. These light weight beauties can double up as a nursing cover, a light blanket, beach wear, a modesty cover for visiting places of worship, and also makes for an enthralling game of peek-a-boo.

12. Learn To Fold Your Garments

Seasoned travellers all swear by rolling their clothes for compact and wrinkle free packing. Bundle packing, where you roll the clothes around a central object as if tying it up, is also a popular method of compact and wrinkle free packing. Stacking folded clothes one on top of another is a big no-no as it makes creases extreme and they are difficult to get rid of without ironing.

13. Wash Your Dirty Laundry

One of the ways to avoid carrying loads of clothes is to wash the clothes you carry. At some places you might get to use the laundry services or a Laundromat but if you are in a pinch, best solution is to wash them yourself. If that is the plan then carrying quick drying clothes is highly recommended, which most often also happen to be the wrinkle free variety.

14. Leave Those Towels Behind

Regular towels take up a lot of space, are heavy and take ages to dry out. If you are staying at hotels they will provide you with towels anyway. If you are travelling to a remote place, where the availability of towels look doubtful, carry a light weight travel towel of viscose material to do the job.

15. Use A Compression Bag

Compression bags are getting lots of recommendation now days from regular travellers. These are useful for saving space in your luggage when you have to pack bulky dresses. While packing for the return trip, get help from the hotel staff to arrange a vacuum cleaner.

Footwear

16. Put On Your Hiking Boots

If you have plans to go hiking or trekking during your trip, you will need those bulky hiking boots. The best way to carry them is to wear them on flight to save space and luggage weight. You can remove the boots once inside and be comfortable in your socks.

17. Picking The Right Shoes

Shoes are often the bulkiest items, along with being the dainty if you are a female. They need care and take up a lot of space in your luggage. It is advisable therefore to pick shoes very carefully. If you plan to do a lot of walking and site seeing, then wearing a pair of comfortable walking shoes are a must. For more formal occasions you can carry durable, light weight flats which will not take up much space.

18. Stuff Shoes

If you happen to pack a pair of shoes, ensure you utilize their hollow insides. Tuck small items like rolled up socks or belts to save space. They will also be easy to find.

Toiletries
19. Stashing Toiletries

Carry only absolute necessities. Airline rules dictate that for one carry-on bag, liquids and gels must be in 3.4 ounce (100ml) bottles or less, and must be packed in a one quart zip-lock bag. If you are planning to stay in a hotel, the basic things will be provided for you. It's best is to buy the rest from the local market at your destination.

20. Take Along Tampons

Tampons are a hard to find item in a lot of countries. Figure out how many you need and pack accordingly. For longer stays you can buy them online and have them delivered to where you are staying.

21. Get Pampered Before You Travel

Some avid travellers suggest getting a pedicure and manicure just the day before travelling. This not only gives you a well kept look, you also save the trouble of packing nail polish. Remember, every little bit of weight reduced adds up.

Electronics
22. Lugging Along Electronics

Electronics have a large role to play in our lives today. Most of us cannot imagine our lives away from our phones, laptops or tablets. However while travelling, one must consider the amount of weight these electronics add to our luggage. Thankfully smart phones come along with all the essentials tools like a camera, email access, picture editing tools and more. They are smart to the point of eliminating the need to carry multiple gadgets. Choose a smart phone that suits all your requirements and travel with the world in your palms or pocket.

23. Reduce the Number of Chargers

If you do travel with multiple electronic devices, you will have to bear the additional burden of carrying all their chargers too. Check if a single charger can be used for multiple devices. You might also consider investing in a pocket charger. These small devices support multiple devices while keeping you charged on the go.

24. Travel Friendly Apps

Along with smart phones come numerous apps, which are immensely helpful in our travels. You name it and you have an app for it at hand – take pictures, sharing with friends and family, torch to light dark roads, maps, checking flight/train times, find hotels and many other things. Use these smart alternatives to traditional items like books to eliminate weight and save space.

I get ideas about what's essential when packing my suitcase.

-Diane von Furstenberg

Travelling With Kids

25. Bring Along the Stroller

Kids might enjoy walking for a while but they soon tire out and a stroller is the just the right thing for them to rest in while you continue your tour. Strollers also double duty as a luggage carrier and shopping bag holder. Remember to pick a light weight, easy to handle brand of stroller. Better yet, find out in advance if you can rent a stroller at your destination.

26. Bring Only Enough Diapers for Your Trip

Diapers take up a lot of space and add to the weight of your luggage. Therefore it is advisable to carry just enough diapers to last through the trip and a few for afterwards, till you buy fresh stock at your destination. Unless of course you are travelling to a really remote area, in which case you have no choice but to carry the load. Otherwise diapers are something you will find pretty easily.

27. Take Only A Couple Of Toys

Children are easily attracted by new things in their environment. While travelling they will find numerous 'new' objects to scrutinize and play with. Packing just one favorite toy is enough, or if there is no favorite toy leave out all of them in favor of stories or imaginary games.

28. Carry Kid Friendly Snacks

Create a small snack counter in your bag to store away quick bites for those sudden hunger pangs. Depending on the child's age this could include chocolates, raisins, dry fruits, granola bars or biscuits. Also keep a bottle of water handy for your little one. These things do not add much weight and can be adjusted in a handbag or knapsack.

29. Games to Carry

Create some travel specific, imaginary games if you have slightly grown up children, like spot the attractions. Keep a coloring book and colors handy for in-flight or hotel time. Apps on your smart phone can keep the children engaged with cartoons and story books. Older children are often entertained by games available on phones or tablets. This cuts the weight of luggage down while keeping the kids entertained.

30. Let the Kids Carry Their Load

A good thing is to start early sharing of responsibilities. Let your child pick a bag of his or her choice and pack it themselves. Keep tabs on what they are stuffing in their bags by asking if they will be using that item on the trip. It could start out being just an entertainment bag initially but with growing years they will learn to sort the useful from the superfluous. Children as little as four can maneuver a small trolley suitcase like a pro- their experience in pull along toys credit. If you are worried that you may be pulling it for them, you may want to start with a backpack.

31. Decide on Location for Children to Sleep

While on a trip you might not always get a crib at your destination, and carrying one will make life all the more difficult. Instead call ahead to see if there are any cribs or roll out beds for children. You may even put blankets on the floor. Weave them a story about camping and they will gladly sleep without any trouble.

32. Get Baby Products Delivered At Your Destination

If you are absolutely paranoid about not getting your favourite variety of diaper or brand of baby food, check out online stores like amazon.com for services in your destination city. You can buy things online ahead of your travel and get them delivered to your hotel upon arrival.

33. Feeding Needs Of Your Infants

If you are travelling with a breastfed infant, you save the trouble of carrying bottles and bottle sanitization kits. For special food, or medications, you may need to call ahead to make sure you have a refrigerator where you are staying.

34. Feeding Needs of Your Toddler

With the progression from infancy to toddler, their dietary requirements too evolve. You will have to pack some snacks for travelling time. Fresh fruits and vegetables can be purchased at your destination. Most of the cities you travel to in whichever part of the world, will have baby food products and formulas, available at the local drug-store or the supermarket.

35. Picking Clothes for Your Baby

Contrary to popular belief, babies can do without many changes of clothes. At the most pack 2 outfits per day. Pack mix and match type clothes for your little one as well. Pick things which are comfortable to wear and quick to dry.

36. Selecting Shoes for Your Baby

Like outfits, kids can make do with two pairs of comfortable shoes. If you can get some water resistant shoes it will be best. To expedite drying wet shoes, you can stuff newspaper in them then wrap them with newspaper and leave them to dry overnight.

37. Keep One Change of Clothes Handy

Travelling with kids can be tricky. Keep a change of clothes for the kids and mum handy in your purse or tote bag. This takes a bit of space in your hand luggage but comes extremely handy in case there are any accidents or spills.

38. Leave Behind Baby Accessories

Baby accessories like their bed, bath tub, car seat, crib etc. should be left at home. Many hotels provide a crib on request, while car seats can be borrowed from friends or rented. Babies can be given a bath in the hotel sink or even in the adult bath tub with a little bit of water. If you bring a few bath toys, they can be used in the bath, pool, and out of water. They can also be sanitized easily in the sink.

39. Carry a Small Load Of Plastic Bags

With children around there are chances of a number of soiled clothes and diapers. These plastic bags help to sort the dirt from the clean inside your big bag. These are very light weight and come in handy to other carry stuff as well at times.

Pack with a Purpose

40. Packing for Business Trips

One neutral-colored suit should suffice. It can be paired with different shirts, ties and accessories for different occasions. One pair of black suit pants could be worn with a matching jacket for the office or with a snazzy top for dinner.

41. Packing for A Cruise

Most cruises have formal dinners, and that formal dress usually takes up a lot of space. However you might find a tuxedo to rent. For women, a short black dress with multiple accessory options will do the trick.

42. Packing for A Long Trip Over Different Climates

The secret packing mantra for travel over multiple climates is layering. Layering traps air around your body creating insulation against the cold. The same light t-shirt that is comfortable in a warmer climate can be the innermost layer in a colder climate.

Reduce Some More Weight

43. Leave Precious Things At Home

Things that you would hate to lose or get damaged leave them at home. Precious jewelry, expensive gadgets or dresses, could be anything. You will not require these on your trip. Leave them at home and spare the load on your mind.

44. Send Souvenirs by Mail

If you have spent all your money on purchasing souvenirs, carrying them back in the same bag that you brought along would be difficult. Either pack everything in another bag and check it in the airport or get everything shipped to your home. Use an international carrier for a secure transit, but this could be more expensive than the checking fees at the airport.

45. Avoid Carrying Books

Books equal to weight. There are many reading apps which you can download on your smart phone or tab. Plus there are gadgets like Kindle and Nook that are thinner and lighter alternatives to your regular book.

Check, Get, Set, Check Again

46. Strategize Before Packing

Create a travel list and prepare all that you think you need to carry along. Keep everything on your bed or floor before packing and then think through once again – do I really need that? Any item that meets this question can be avoided. Remove whatever you don't really need and pack the rest.

47. Test Your Luggage

Once you have fully packed for the trip take a test trip with your luggage. Take your bags and go to town for window shopping for an hour. If you enjoy your hour long trip it is good to go, if not, go home and reduce the load some more. Repeat this test till you hit the right weight.

48. Add a Roll Of Duct Tape

You might wonder why, when this book has been talking about reducing stuff, we're suddenly asking you to pack something totally unusual. This is because when you have limited supplies, duct tape is immensely helpful for small repairs – a broken bag, leaking zip-lock bag, broken sunglasses, you name it and duct tape can fix it, temporarily.

49. List of Essential Items

Even though the emphasis is on packing light, there are things which have to be carried for any trip. Here is our list of essentials:

- Passport/Visa or any other ID

- Any other paper work that might be required on a trip like permits, hotel reservation confirmations etc.

- Medicines – all your prescription medicines and emergency kit, especially if you are travelling with children

- Medical or vaccination records

- Money in foreign currency if travelling to a different country

- Tickets- Email or Message them to your phone

50. Make the Most of Your Trip

Wherever you are going, whatever you hope to do we encourage you to embrace it whole-heartedly. Take in the scenery, the culture and above all, enjoy your time away from home.

On a long journey even a straw weighs heavy.

-Spanish Proverb

Packing and Planning Tips

A Week before Leaving

- Arrange for someone to take care of pets and water plants

- Stop mail and newspaper

- Notify Credit Card companies where you are going.

- Change your thermostat settings

- Car inspected, oil is changed, and tires have the correct pressure.

- Passports and id is up to date.

- Pay bills.

- Copy important items and download travel Apps.

- Start collecting small bills for tips

Right Before Leaving

- Clean out refrigerator.

- Empty garbage cans.

- Lock windows.

- Make sure you have the right ID with you.

- Bring cash for tips.

- Remember travel documents.

- Lock door behind you.

- Remember wallet.

- Unplug items in house and pack chargers.

>TOURIST

Read other
Greater Than a Tourist
Books

Greater Than a Tourist San Miguel de Allende Guanajuato Mexico:
50 Travel Tips from a Local by Tom Peterson

Greater Than a Tourist – Lake George Area New York USA:
 50 Travel Tips from a Local by Janine Hirschklau

Greater Than a Tourist – Monterey California United States:
50 Travel Tips from a Local by Katie Begley

 Greater Than a Tourist – Chanai Crete Greece:
50 Travel Tips from a Local by Dimitra Papagrigoraki

Greater Than a Tourist – The Garden Route Western Cape Province
South Africa:
50 Travel Tips from a Local by Li-Anne McGregor van Aardt

Greater Than a Tourist – Sevilla Andalusia Spain:
50 Travel Tips from a Local by Gabi Gazon

Greater Than a Tourist – Kota Bharu Kelantan Malaysia:
50 Travel Tips from a Local by Aditi Shukla

Children's Book: Charlie the Cavalier Travels the World by Lisa
Rusczyk

>TOURIST

> TOURIST

Visit Greater Than a Tourist for Free Travel Tips
http://GreaterThanATourist.com

Sign up for the Greater Than a Tourist Newsletter for
discount days, new books, and travel information:
http://eepurl.com/cxspyf

Follow us on Facebook for tips, images, and ideas:
https://www.facebook.com/GreaterThanATourist

Follow us on Pinterest for travel tips and ideas:
http://pinterest.com/GreaterThanATourist

Follow us on Instagram for beautiful travel images:
http://Instagram.com/GreaterThanATourist

>TOURIST

> TOURIST

Please leave your honest review of this book on Amazon and Goodreads. Please send your feedback to GreaterThanaTourist@gmail.com as we continue to improve the series. Thank you. We appreciate your positive and constructive feedback. Thank you.

>TOURIST

NOTES

Printed in Great Britain
by Amazon

26076309R00067